Fifty Shades
of
Shopping
Un-gagged

Mark Taylor

Mark Taylor

ISBN-13:
978-1499635898

ISBN-10:
1499635893

DEDICATION

To my mother and father who convinced me that trying
was the first step on the road to succeeding.

Mark Taylor

CONTENTS

ACKNOWLEDGMENTS

Thanks to all the salespeople and buyers I have had the privilege to work with over the years.

Only you will know what a roller coaster our chosen professions can be, and only you will know how much fun you can have when you get it right.

It is not intended to encourage illegal and negative behaviour. Remember, laws vary around the world and the consequences of breaking them can be extreme for you and your business. If you believe you or your company may be conducting business illegally you should immediately consult a local expert.

Tactical behaviour in negotiations often reduces the value of deals instead of increasing it.

PROLOGUE

So let's start with a question. Why should you give a rats arse about this book? Well it`s because it is about your money.

Each day billions of dollars change hands around the world in retail stores or online and this money starts its journey in your pocket.

When you decide to give some of your hard earned, in return for a product or service, it is the culmination of an extraordinary series of events some of which are worthy of their own mini series. Deception, lies, physical abuse, sex, blackmail and intimidation. All of these are the *plat du jour* for some retailers and manufacturers of branded consumer packaged goods also know as Fast Moving Consumer Goods (FMCG). Basically the stuff in your weekly shopping basket.

Huge multi billion dollar businesses pull stunts that

are the equivalent of pointing in the air and shouting "what's that?", and then snatching the other persons handbag and running away as soon as they look up.

These amazing tactics are part of the world of retail buying and selling.

Each day negotiation meetings are held around the world in which dirty tricks are dressed up as a partnership.

Amazingly, most of the participants post rationalise what they are doing to each other. They can't admit what actually happens and how their behaviour would be viewed if it was broadcast as part of a TV reality show. The outrage, court cases and long sentences would make headlines around the world.

It`s interesting that many of the characters, in this real life play, particularly value; honesty and trust. It still doesn't stop them cheating and swindling their way through life.

Don`t believe that I advocate this type of behaviour. I have spent much of my life teaching people how to deal with it. It still doesn't stop me occasionally laughing out loud so hard it has me reaching for the Tena Lady. Some of the outrageous stunts people pull, in the name of generating profit for their businesses and advancing their careers, are at a very simple level, but others are truly world class.

This book lifts the lid on some classic and some highly advanced ways that retailers and manufacturers extract as much value as possible out of every single transaction. And it`s all in the name of satisfying you, the consumer. Basically all this bad behaviour is your fault.

I have completely ignored the good behaviour that takes place. Let's face it, watching buyers and sellers skip hand in hand, through flower filled meadows towards the sunset, would be pretty boring. Instead I have focused on behaviours that are less than pleasant. The sneaky, the devious, the dark. Basically, the ones that are really interesting.

In major retailers around the world the standard of training buying teams are given is extraordinary, especially when you compare it to the average manufacturer or supplier. Not only do they have their management and commercial skills developed but they are also taught highly advanced purchasing strategies. In fact you will learn a few that will make you a mint in your private life if you use them properly.

In addition to this the mentality, driven from senior management, regarding the expectations surrounding delivery of value to the business and the consequences of failure, are extreme.

Historically, Monday morning meetings for retail commercial teams, where the previous weeks trade was analysed, were legendary. Senior Directors wouldn't think twice about verbally tearing Managers to shreds in public if they weren't hitting the numbers.

Buying teams are trained to bring the maximum

benefit to a retailer that enables them to remain competitive in the fight for shopper *share of pocket* (the disposable income in your bank account).

So if you are a salesperson, this book will help you recognise the strategies you are actually dealing with during your meetings and it gives some simple advice to follow.

For buyers, it may highlight a new *legal* way to increase the profit for your company.

And if you are a shopper, you will get more from each trip knowing the hilarious games that are played in the name of meeting your ever increasing demands.

This book is a sometimes funny look at how far buyers can go to squeeze every last drop of cash from major branded suppliers around the world and the behaviour this produces in sales teams.

It is not a *how to guide* but a short, punchy, look at examples of the secret tactics and mindset professional buyers can use to drive their businesses in the name of satisfying you the shopper.

1 SUPPLIER MANAGEMENT
OR
"SOMETIMES IT'S OK TO BRING A KNIFE TO A GUNFIGHT"

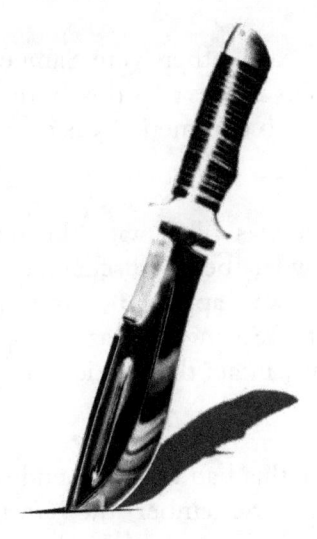

On September 19th 1827, two men met on a sandbar just outside Natchez, Mississippi.

They had come to resolve a disagreement and, in a traditionally rational manner of the time, decided that trying to blow each others heads off in a duel would be the perfect way to achieve this.

Facing each other were Samuel Levi Wells III and Dr. Thomas Harris Maddox both holding pistols. The instruction to commence was given and each man took two shots.

The air was filled with the thick, acrid stench of black powder being discharged and, as the smoke cleared, it was apparent that both had missed their opponent! Seeing this as an opportunity to escape with dignity intact they decided to shake hands and call it quits.

Now if this had been the end of the matter no one would ever remember the *Great Sandbar Dual* but things didn't finish that simply. Supporting each man was over a dozen individuals who also had issues to settle.

Colonel Crain, who was there in support of

Maddox, was first to fire at an adversary named Cuny. The first shot went wide and struck another man in the hip, knocking him to the ground. After a further exchange of gunfire Cuny lay dead from a chest wound.

Now this could also have been the end of the dispute apart from one simple fact, the man that was struck in the hip by the wayward shot was Jim Bowie, one of the toughest characters alive. Strapped to his hip was his, soon to be famous, Bowie knife.

He drew it and charged headlong at Crain who hit Bowie so hard across the head with his gun that it broke. Bowie fell to his knees stunned.

In the background Major Norris Wright, an old enemy of Bowie's, decided now was as good a time as any to end their personal feud.

Summoning up all his courage, which doesn't seem to be much as his target was nearly unconscious in front of him, he pulled out his pistol and fired but missed the stricken Bowie.

Not to let the opportunity go Wright drew his sword cane and stabbed Bowie in the chest.

Here is where things went badly wrong for Wright, excuse the pun. If you are squeamish you may want to skip the next few paragraphs.

Talk to any good knife maker and they will tell you that there can be an issue with using a blade as a stabbing weapon. The combination of the blood and flesh, which the blade goes into, can create a vacuum with the metal and make it very difficult withdraw.

This is exactly what happened to Wright. The blade was stuck firmly in Bowies chest and, in attempt to retrieve it, Wright did something spectacularly stupid. He put his foot on Bowie and pulled.

The benefit, for anyone using a sword in hand to hand combat versus using a knife, is simple. A sword has a longer reach and allows you to inflict damage to your opponent before they get near enough to do it to you. Wright had now given up this tactical advantage and the injured Bowie made him pay for his error.

Bowie grabbed Wright`s shirt and pulled him forward, straight onto the lethal blade of Bowies huge hunting knife.

Wright was disembowelled and died immediately.

Around Bowie other men, loyal to Wright, began shooting. He was hit again and then stabbed but he made it to his feet. Now he began to draw out Wrights sword, which was still protruding from his chest.

Two brothers, Cary and Alfred Blanchard, took advantage of the moment and fired.

Bowie took yet another bullet, this time in the arm. Spinning around, he lashed out and sliced off part of Alfred's forearm scaring the brothers so much that they ran off firing wildly but missing Bowie.

In the ten minutes the fight lasted two men lost their lives and four others, including Bowie, were injured.

Why am I telling you this story when I am supposed to be letting you into the secret games that are played by retailers and manufacturers in an attempt to make a profit.

It`s simple. Buyers are always in Bowies position, they bring a knife to a gunfight.

When they have to deal with manufacturers who have high loyalty brands, which shoppers want, they are always in a weaker position.

They know that if they don't stock these products then shoppers will just start buying their supplies at competitors stores. The retailer effectively loses a customer and all of their annual household spend. It`s a huge problem!

This is especially true when the market place is tough and stores are fighting for every penny of profit they can. Losing shoppers in this environment can be financially catastrophic and it makes it virtually impossible, for buyers of even the largest companies in the world, to cut better deals.

In these negotiations you would, therefore, think it was a blood bath, with buyers bodies festooning the ground. Salespeople should be riding the range sporting many scalps on their belt, metaphorically speaking of course, but that's not actually the case.

In fact it's the other way around much of the time. Like Bowie, buyers don't understand the idea that it's an impossible game to win. Negotiation is as much about mental attitude as anything.

I see people, the world over, teach sales teams how to negotiate. It's a subject I hold dear to my heart. They show them the techniques and processes. What you cannot teach easily is the mental conditioning experts have. The ability to look into someone with steel cold eyes and know that you have the worst cards at the table but will still walk away with everything you want, plus the shirt off their back.

This takes time to develop in most people and some will never quite make it.

Buyers often back up their skills with a simple, but spectacularly powerful process, to make certain that they keep manufacturers under control. In fact, it's the same process many people use naturally in their personal lives with a partner.

If someone should feel that they are being taken for granted in a relationship it starts to eat away at them.

To make a point they may start becoming distant with their other half. Perhaps reducing interpersonal interaction, often arguing even when they do talk and maybe even withholding sex.

Its is beautifully characterised by the "fine" conversation.

Question: "You don't seem very happy, are you ok?"
Answer: "Fine."

Now many of us have been in this situation and we know that the last thing the other person is is "fine". So what do they do? Pay more attention? Make more effort? Maybe even buy flowers etc?

Retailers have exactly the same behaviour if they think they are not getting the best service and deals.

It can manifest itself in many ways. For instance, lots of painful issues start arising. Calls from the salespeople to the retailer are not returned. Maybe promotional opportunities go to another supplier for no good reason.

What is the retail equivalent of withholding sex? Some of your products get delisted in favour of competitors or new products fail to be listed immediately.

Sometimes, as suppliers get closer to a retail buyer and relationships improve, life for the supplier can get too comfortable. This isn't in the interest of a retailer because the manufacturer will stop trying as hard. They take the situation for granted. So what do retailers do in response to this?

Often it is as simple as changing the buyer. One minute you are dealing with a person who is buying cosmetics and the next minute you are dealing with someone who was buying potatoes yesterday. Instantly the relationship has gone. It often isn't because they have greater expertise it might simply be because they can walk through the door and say the magic words "If you want to keep doing business you are going to have to work a lot harder than you did for the last buyer".

Salespeople want to make a good impression so out comes the commercial equivalent of a bunch of flowers. This will be better promotions, improved terms, more advertising support... ...you get the idea.

Try it yourself. If you are in a personal relationship get one person to negotiate the best price they can for a new house, car, whatever. Then, when that person has got as far as they can, walk away to consider it and then switch to the other person. You will always get a little more. You should try to negotiate everything you buy of reasonable value, it's like a pay increase and it's a lot of fun. I just bought the new PlayStation for my son. You wouldn't believe the deal I managed on a product that people can't get enough stock of, just by asking for more.

Some retailers use this process of disrupting the relationship instinctively. Other companies may, on a periodic basis, actually plan how and when they will do this. Every eighteen months to two years seems to be a sweet spot, but suppliers with annual terms have actually *annualised* this process.

Every year, before next years negotiations start, the business seems to come off the rails for no good reason.

Everything is just so difficult for you and your competitors seem to be winning the game.

In fact, however hard you work, nothing is going right and you are continually getting your arse kicked.

Rule 1:   As a man once said, *just because you are paranoid doesn't mean they aren't out to get you.*   Listen to your instincts.   If you think more money can solve the problems you`re encountering with your customer it is probably a good sign you are being *managed* by your buyer.   You are actually in a game of poker, not looking after the day to day business.

You may be facing the commercial equivalent of Jim Bowie. The best buyers have the skill, tenacity and mental strength, to stand in a gunfight with a knife and still come out alive.

Just make certain they don't leave with your scalp.

2 CYCLICAL TERMS REALIGNMENT
OR
"LET ME HELP YOU, HELP ME, HELP YOU... ...HELP ME"

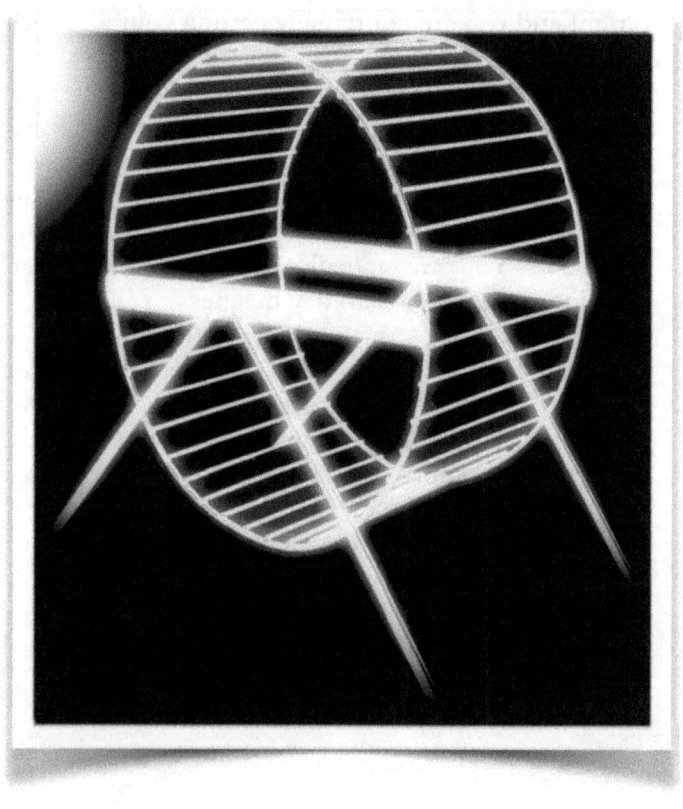

The salesperson sat opposite the buyer.

Both were surrounded by an ocean of paper crowding in on their laptops.

It was the end of year consolidation of support payments and both of them had had enough. The meeting had gone on for hours as the disputes over relatively small amounts of money were slowly resolved.

The buyer let out a long breath that carried, both the smell of a dozen cups of coffee in addition to, the frustration he was feeling.

"There has to be a better way to go on than this, I can't see us doing as much business next year, you are just making it too hard" he said.

"Look, I feel exactly the same way but what else can we do? The salesman replied. "We need to track incentives and so far we have only had a few discrepancies"

The buyer let his head fall onto the paper pile closest to him with a solid thud and then proceeded to bang it gently into the desk as he spoke. "I... bump ...get... bump ...that... bump ...but... bump ...it... bump ...is... bump ...killing... bump ...your... bump ...chances... bump ...of... bump ...

doing... bump ...more... bump ...business... bump." After the last solid connection he just left it on the table.

The salesperson stared at him as if he had completely lost the plot.

In his mind he had a vivid mental image of himself, helping the buyers head on its way onto the desk with a firmly placed swing of a cricket bat. He shook himself out of his sociopathic fantasy. "Ok but what is the option? If we don't pay any incentives you'll give our competitors all of the space we have and our business will die".

The buyer slowly lifted his head. He was smiling. If cats could smile they would have the same expression on their faces just as they are about to eat the family budgie. "That`s a good question. You know, I think I have an idea..." He said licking his lips.

Between every manufacturer and retailer there is a set of trade terms under which products are supplied, and these cover many different elements.

In this chapter I just want to focus on pricing incentives that manufacturers offer and not the million other things they end up paying for.

When you walk into a supermarket and see a price ticket on the shelf you don't see the huge amount of mathematics, discussions, arguments and analytics that have gone into producing it.

Typically, terms can be made up of list price, invoice price, trade discounts, retrospective targets, growth targets, ranging incentives, distribution incentives, the list goes on and on.

Manufacturers use these to encourage retailers to increase the amount of products which are bought from them, and hopefully grow profits. This isn't always the case though.

Over the course of many years annual terms negotiations, these incentives can get very complicated, especially when they differ from one range of products to the next.

So how do buyers use this complication to improve their bottom line?

Firstly they encourage manufacturers to add more and more incentives, ideally just to maintain the current range. Yes this sounds crazy but in an aggressive market place it is easy to feel the pressure from competitors, and be persuaded that your current range is under threat.

For many buyers this is the easiest way to avoid an annual price increase. They just allow a manufacturer to believe their existing range is under threat.

In that way salespeople often decide to delay an annual price increase or, better still for the retailer, not to increase prices at all as a sign of *goodwill* (of course on the understanding that the current range is maintained in full).

Basically the manufacturer negotiates with

themselves. It`s based completely on the little nagging voices in their head, planted by a few well timed comments from the buyer.

A buyer simply saying "We are under extreme pressure to remain competitive in this category next year" will often be met with a sales director panicking and falling straight into the trap by thinking "there is no way we can risk increasing prices this year".

If pressed, a buyer simply has to shrug their shoulders and say nothing to erode the corporate confidence of even the largest manufacturers.

The target for many buyers is to actually introduce more complexity into the terms and add in new discount structures.

After a couple of years of this the terms get so difficult to track that a simple solution is suggested by the buyer. **Consolidate all the old terms and make them off invoice discounts!**

What this does is take away the requirement for a retailer to perform to receive its maximum discount. *Money for old rope* I think this is what it`s called.

Buyers may say spurious comments like "it is impossible to see what your products earn in our business because we do not track all the discounts like you do" or "These discounts go into the marketing budget and do not directly show against your products at all". Either way it looks like a great idea to get rid of all the separate performance related discounts and just reduce the price.

Alternatively they get rolled into one annual volume target (which is nearly as bad).

But what happens six months later when the buyer asks for a payment for bringing in a new product and wants a *new* volume discount? The salesperson will get upset and say this money is already included in the net price but the buyer tells them *the competition will pay for the space,* so if they want the product listed they will have to pay too. After all, that's only fair!

The discounts increase and then, in 18 months time, it gets complicated and here we go again.

We are on the big hamster wheel of terms negotiation.

Rule 2: Never introduce a discount, under any circumstances, that isn't conditional and doesn't require the retailer to perform better. Never. Ever. It's not a sign of good will, relationship building, or investing for the future. It's a sign you have been had. And yes, they will laugh their rear ends off at their team meeting.

I am sorry to be this harsh but it`s important to feel the pain.   If you realised how often buyers boast internally about the stunts they get away with, more salespeople would get indignant about how they were treated and push back.

3 RATE CARDS
OR
"NEGOTIATION BY LASER PRINTER"

So beyond normal discounts there are a massive array of items manufacturers will end up paying for as part of their support for a retailer.

Everything from payment days to discounts and from marketing investments to staff training are negotiated.

In fact you could be shocked at what some manufacturers pay for to support retailers. In my career I have come across manufacturers paying for all the following:

Payment terms which allow a retailer to receive and sell the goods but not have to pay the bill for several months (basically they become the

retailers bank).

The wages for shop floor staff.

Shelf space to place their products.

The fixtures the products go on.

Staff training.

Administration charges to list a new product.

Electricity to power freezer units.

Lighting above a display.

Staff Christmas parties by buying a supplier table.

Category captaincy (often the chance to give manufacturer data and planning resource for free).

Lunches.

Dinners.

Breakfasts.

Travel costs.

Posters.

Price tickets on the shelf.

Delivery.

Failure to deliver penalties.

Late delivery penalties.

Delivery penalties!   Wrong invoice details, wrong quantities etc.

Meetings with buyers.

Promotions.

Advertising.

Being boring.

Looking ugly...

Basically they invent any manner of rubbish to charge a manufacturer.

And the crazy thing? Manufacturers pay for it!

Twenty years ago retailers payed for their own rent, bought shelves to put product on, developed their own promotions, payed for their own logistics, printed their own point of sale and staffed the stores with their own teams.

Now, every cost that can be imagined gets passed onto manufacturers.

I remember, in my last days as head of a buying team, mentioning to a manufacturer how much the fleet of company cars for my buyers cost.

Within minutes we were discussing utilising their fleet car discounts to reduce costs.

An unscrupulous buyer would have had them paying for some of the vehicles as part of the running costs of managing their products.

Of course, I`m a commercial saint, and therefore wouldn't do anything as underhand as that. For many buying teams though, it is a great game to work out new ways they can extract additional support from manufacturers.

In fact, it is something to be bragged about behind closed doors for many retail teams.

How do they make these imaginary items appear real? It's simple. They buy a laser printer.

It seems that if it is in print it is real. An account

manager handed a piece of official looking paper with a table of costs on it believes it to be the truth.

In fact you can get more credibility by faxing it or mailing it with a short note saying simply "Enclosed our new marketing rate chart for suppliers effective immediately". For some reason many companies treat it as if Moses had delivered it, carved on tablets of stone, in Gods own handwriting. The fact that it was typed in 5 minutes and filled with random numbers selected by the rule of "Do you really think they will fall for this one" is irrelevant.

$15,000 to list a new product, $50,000 to have branded displays, $100,000 to advise on a product sector $1,000,000 to be a global partner. It`s unbelievable. The really funny thing is that *all* of these items make more money anyway by helping sell additional product, but manufacturers still pay!

Many salespeople feel it doesn't seem right but they still end up agreeing to it without much of a struggle.

Buddha is quoted as saying "Do not believe in anything simply because you have heard it. Do not believe in anything simply because it is spoken and rumoured by many. Do not believe in anything simply because it is found written in your religious books. Do not believe in anything merely on the authority of your teachers and elders. Do not believe in traditions because they have been handed down for many generations. But after observation and analysis, when you find that anything agrees with reason and is conducive

to the good and benefit of one and all, then accept it and live up to it."

It is one of his most famous quotes found on the internet and is used by people to illustrate the importance of remaining a free thinking individual.

The funny thing is that he never said it. It`s a fake.

So it sort of proves the point that, just because it is in writing, it is not necessarily the truth. Before we get into a theological debate, on what truth actually is, lets keep life simple.

Rule 3: If it has four legs like a dog, wags it's tail like a dog and barks like a dog, it's a dog. It's definitely not a cat with a cough.

Do not fall for taking on costs without getting a significant return for your own business. A real return, not a mystical, magical, promise, of future riches that will be delivered strapped to a golden Unicorn called Frank.

4 FISHING FOR FUNDS
OR
"HAND ME DOWN THE SHOVEL, THIS HOLE ISN'T DEEP ENOUGH YET"

One of the crucial needs most salespeople feel they have to satisfy is to be liked by, or even better, become friends with a buyer. Their company, their bosses and even their peers often judge an account managers success, not just by the profit they generate, but the relationship they engender in a buyer. It`s like getting an Alligator as a pet. Very exciting but inherently dangerous.

Why do they want to develop a good relationship? It's simple. It's the same reason some guys want to make a good impression with women. Because they want something. Salespeople want to sell more of their product at a better price. This sounds cynical but it's true. Most salespeople choke on the words, when you ask them about their motives, and they give wonderful testaments to trust, rapport and respect, but after a bit of probing the reality comes into sharp focus. They actually just want to get things on their own terms and a positive relationships helps.

The problem is that buyers hear the same story all the time and this hardens them to the commercial chat up lines they are served daily.

Now I am going to start with a gross generalisation. My life, for most of the last decade, has been spent teaching negotiation to teams around the world. The one thing I've realised is that women are, on average, better natural negotiators than men. Here is my (probably misguided) idea of why this is.

If a guy stands at a bar and a pretty girl walks in, stands next to him, looks him up and down, and then compliments him on what a great suit he is wearing. In his mind he is saying "yes, you are right, I look good in this outfit. Thanks for noticing the effort I made. By the way would you like a drink?".

If the roles are reversed and the same thing happens to a girl she will typically think "what are you after?"

This is because she has had the same conversation a thousand times. Much like professional buyers.

Sorry men, it's just a fact. The good news is it doesn't mean you can't be as good, or even better, you just start from a lower level because your ability to spot social bullshit is not as highly tuned.

So how does this translate into strategies a buyer will use to extract more value from manufacturers? Well over the course of this book I will give a few examples of classic ways buyers use this to their advantage, along with many other tactics that are part of their secret armoury.

Let me tell you a story as a start on the road, and believe me it is not an isolated incident. These things happen every day.

I've had an unusual life, having held roles both in buying and selling. When I first moved over, from managing an account for a manufacturer to running the buying team for a retailer, I was shocked by the lengths to which sales people go in an attempt at ingratiating themselves with their customers.

Often they would grasp at straws to find some common ground which would provide the basis for building a relationship. The lowest common denominator for guys was always sport. Shoot me if I ever again get asked *what soccer team do you support* or *did you see the match last night*. It's nice to have a chat but when you are really busy it just winds people up. Especially as you know they couldn't care less much of the time, and they really just want to sell you something.

Actually the subject we had in common was *how are we going to make more money for our businesses in the future?* This was often, frustratingly, the last topic covered.

So, if salespeople feel the need to build a relationship to help them achieve their objective, the easiest way for a buyer to take control of the situation is to use it to their advantage. This sounds very manipulative but the tactics professional buyers are taught, and to be fair, the social skills most people use naturally, are often manipulative.

By the way, don't get too pious thinking you are any different. There have been many studies on the subject and the results vary but, in most new social situations where a conversation takes place, people lie on average 3 times in the first 10 minutes. Ask yourself when you last used a *white lie* rather than upset someone (and I bet it was in the last 24 hours).

This dinner tastes really good.
I love your new haircut.
This is lovely, what a pretty crayon drawing.
I don`t mind you calling me at the weekend boss, actually I was really bored and appreciate the extra work I have to do now.

Why do you do it? To be accepted socially? To be liked? This is the same for salespeople but, with them, money and their job are on the line.

Men, apparently, lie on average 6 times per day and women 3. This seems very low to me. After years working on body language and verbal signals, particularly ones that show if someone`s probably lying, I would quadruple these numbers when working in a business environment.

By nature, mankind is manipulative. Put money in the equation and it gets far worse. Commercial negotiation is best described as *corporate poker,* where hands are played out using mind games as much as facts. The pots at stake can run into hundreds of millions of dollars over a specific contract period.

Ok so now we understand the basis for many meetings that take place between manufacturers of big brands and the retailers that stock them. They are filled with smiling faces that hide self interest on both sides.

This particular story shows how easily salespeople can get into trouble when they step onto the thin ice created by a business relationship.

A few months after I started managing a retail buying team, I was asked by a colleague to sit in on a meeting with a new account manager. The request was to *glad hand* them a little. Specifically, to show how much they were valued and also to encourage their continued support of our business.

The new salesperson was frothing with enthusiasm about meeting someone he viewed as part of the senior team. I guess he looked forward to reporting back to his boss that he was already making great connections with the new guy.

To be fair to him, he had done his homework well. He had found out I also used to be an account manager, looking after one of the retailers in the industry.

In fact we had something else in common because he had also looked after the same account. We laughed about *the old days* and ran through names of a few people we both new.

"Who was the blond lady buyer with the unusual last name?" He asked.

I knew exactly the one he meant. She was known in the industry as *The Rottweiler*. It had been my unfortunate task to sell to her for a period of time. She was very professional but had a well deserved reputation for being extremely tough.

"Alyson Parmenter" I said. Sensing he had a personal opinion about her I dangled a hook. "She was a real piece of work." I continued.

Realising we had some new common ground he followed my lead.

"Boy was she" he said "what a complete bitch!"

"You know her well" I said.

"Oh yes," he volunteered "she was a nightmare. Any idea where she is working now? She disappeared off the map a couple of years ago."

"Yes I do in fact." I replied lifting my arm and looking at my watch. "Right now she is probably giving our son his lunchtime bottle".

I could see a word forming in his mind. The word was *Bollocks*. He went a shade of white I`ve never seen in a live human face before. Beside me the buyer, who was my wife`s friend, was barely able to stop herself exploding with laughter.

With a stoney face I got up. I explained I had to go to another meeting and walked out of the room, accompanied by my colleague. As the door closed we disintegrated laughing. "What do you want me to do?" she asked.

"Skin him and fry him" I replied.

As it turned out she didn't have to do anything.

Because salespeople *need* to build relationships he flagellated himself like a monk after watching a Miley Cyrus concert.

Over the course of the meeting the he busted his stitches to prove how important the business was to him, how sorry he was, and that he would go the extra mile to apologise. All of this effort was worth big money to us, at a time when we needed it and, better still, it established the buyer as the dominant character in this business relationship.

Actually he was right. When it was required my wife could be tough, and if you did something really stupid she could be far worse. His value judgement though, without knowing the facts, cost him. Buyers dangle these conversations in front of salespeople and seem to have a sixth sense when they know someone`s about to fall down a huge hole.

It doesn't happen by accident. Sometimes they didn't fall down the hole. Sometimes they were pushed.

Ask any account manager and most of them will have an "I can't believe I said that" moment to confess. Buy me a beer and I can tell you some of mine. I have some really cringe making ones.

Rule 4: No Subjective Comments. It`s the same as playing Russian Roulette. Eventually you'll find a loaded chamber and blow your own brains out (or wished you had).

Think of selling and buying in the same way you would dating. Asking loads of questions, rather than making statements, is a better way of getting to understand the other person and to build a solid relationship.

If you do get pushed down a dirty great hole just smile and say "wow, I really fell for that one" and climb out.

5 CHANGE THE POLICY
OR
"THE FIVE O'CLOCK FREDDY"

Part of my career has allowed me to work with some really interesting businesses, and see some amazing tactics used first hand.

For most of the last decade I have taught sales teams how to deal with these tactics during negotiations, and one spectacular event occurred during one of these courses.

It's Monday morning and I arrive at the offices of a very large supplier based in Europe. I have been asked to teach some of the key accounts team and arrive at 8am to set up.

As I enter the offices it's obvious that something is not right with the world. People are running back and forth with panicky looks on their faces. I had once, unwittingly, parked next to a terrorist bomb hidden in a telephone box in London. As the people were evacuated from the streets they had similar expressions to some of the ones I was seeing now.

By the time it got to 8:30, start time of the event, I was still standing in an empty room. Finally I saw a face I recognised. One of the national accounts team, that I had previously met before, put her head around the door and explained they needed a little more time.

Apparently the executive team had asked for some urgent information.

"Ok that's fine but what's the issue?" I asked "It seems very serious."

She proceeded to tell me an amazing story.

On the previous Friday they had received a *Five o'clock Freddy!*

A Five o'clock Freddy is named after an old colleague of mine. Freddy was notorious for going AWOL (absent without leave) during the working week only to arrive back in the office just before five on a Friday afternoon. He then caused so much disruption, during the hour he graced us with his presence, that people ended up working most of the weekend to fix the problems.

Needless to say Freddy was as welcome as a tin tack in a balloon factory.

He also became the nickname for any unnatural disaster that turned up out of the blue.

The Freddy that this company received came in the form of a fax. It was from the biggest retail customer this supplier had and, paraphrased, it went roughly like this.

"Dear Sirs, we are currently conducting a supplier evaluation by a team of consultants. In the next few weeks you will be notified if you are a core business partner, general supplier or no longer a supplier to our stores". It continued "In the meantime please accept our new policy which states our terms for supply (attached) under which all new orders will be placed."

Behind this simple cover sheet was a thick wad of finely printed terms and conditions. It meant a million dollar increase was required in their support for the retailer without any increased business offered in return.

This was sent to a supplier that had been in a, theoretical, partnership with this retailer for decades.

The "new policy" move is a classic tactic that rewrites the rules of the game. Even if a supplier doesn't accept all of them, the retailer will normally get something as a way of placating their customer.

Rule 5: Manufacturers set the terms of supply, not the retailer. Any changes to that are a negotiation. It is important that value for the manufacturer should also be added when value for the retailer is increased.

Anything else feels closer to highway robbery. Salespeople may want to remind them that Dick Turpin had the common decency to wear a mask when he held up the stagecoach. Maybe handing them one at the meeting might diffuse a confrontational situation and get everyone laughing instead of arguing.

Allowing terms to be dictated is the equivalent of letting a five year old decide what they can eat for dinner and being surprised that they have a plate piled high with sweets.

For this manufacturing company this fax had meant most of the team working over the weekend. They spent their time trying to decide what they could afford to give and how they should phrase the official reply.

My suggestion was that a simple text with the word *No,* sent on the Friday, would have saved a lot wasted time.

As it turned out this is what eventually happened several weeks later, but it was after even more useless attempts at making logical sense of a totally illogical request.

Typically, Five o'clock Freddy's land on a Friday, as close to the close of business as possible, because that's when they have the most impact.

If something devastating lands in your inbox at the end of the week, or your mobile rings between 3 and 5pm and it's *an emergency* not of your making, you are probably in receipt of a Freddy.

My suggestion is use the same level of enthusiasm to deal with your Freddy as we did with ours.

The Freddy I knew was *accidentally* run over by members of his team and then secretly buried in the foundations of the new office block being built next door. Honestly. Would I lie to you? I'm a buyer. Trust me.

6 COMPETITION THREATS
OR
"BEWARE THE PEOPLE IN THE WOODS"

When I was small, and believe me I am going back a long way, I had my fair share of nightmares.

Apart from the usual array of monsters, night terrors and, of course, clowns, there was one thing that could guarantee waking me up, and making me stare desperately into the shadows to see if anything was lurking there.

The people in the woods.

These were not real people, and they did not necessarily live in the woods, but that was what made them so terrifying.

I didn't really know what they were, where they lived, or what they looked like. I just knew they were there. Somewhere. And I think they had long teeth and sharp claws.

What really made my skin crawl was that they were completely shapeless.

It was that fear of the unknown which was so powerful. Insidiously, it crept inside my imagination and my own mind began creating terrors that Stephen King would be proud of.

It's not a fear of the dark but a fear of what's hidden by the dark.

Buyers are great friends with *the people in the woods*. If fact these creatures help buyers get what they want.

They also know that their other biggest ally is the mind of the salesperson.

To a supplier *the people in the woods* are their nearest competitors.

Always suspicious, salespeople continuously look for clues as to what strategy a competitor is using to take part of their current business.

In fact, legislation helps the buyer too. It is illegal, in many countries, for one manufacturer to call another and discuss trading plans with their competitors. So if a buyer allowed a salesperson to think they were uncompetitive, even though they had the lowest price in the market, there is no simple way to legally find out.

It requires little effort to start the night terrors with *the people in the woods*. Just a few well chosen words and bingo! The mind of the salesperson takes over, and now they themselves start imagining all the sharp teeth and claws closing in on them.

Phrases like "So you really believe this is a competitive price in this market?" or "Everyone else is investing ahead of the curve if they want to survive next year" place just enough doubt in the head of an account manager to make them start working out ways to improve the renumeration for retailers.

Seriously, what the hell sense does "investing ahead of the curve" or "investing in our future partnership" actually mean?

Honestly it`s mostly "give me money in the hope we will do more business with you in the future".   It makes no commercial sense at all but it works because *the people in the woods* are doing it, so you must too (or their claws will be into you).

Rule 6: *The people in the woods* are only as scary as you allow them to be.

How did I get rid of the nightmares when I was six? I turned on the light. They vanished immediately.

How can you, metaphorically, turn on the light in commercial meetings?

Tell them the story about the frightening nights young kids have and the terrors that fill their minds. Then, look straight into their eyes, smile, and say "are you trying to scare me with *the people in the woods* too?"

7 OVER RANGING
OR
"DOES MY BUM LOOK BIG IN THIS?"

There are two, truly terrifying, questions that any man can be asked.

"Is it always this size" is probably not good to hear but the one that is so frightening and makes *the people in the woods* seem like a bunch of Girl Scouts is "Do I look fat in this dress?"

Assuming you are in the worst position possible and she actually does look like the equivalent of a baby hippopotamus in spandex you may want to take the easy way out and bite down hard on your cyanide filled rear molar.

If your father was not as forward thinking as mine and he did not give you one as a wedding present then you are pretty much stuffed.

There is no answer to this that will not have significant consequences at some time. It may be years ahead but I can guarantee this conversation will be played back in all its glory.

So what do you do? Be honest and say *yes* to save her from public embarrassment or say *no* and show you *love the way she looks good no matter what she wears,* and effectively take the cowards way out?

Lie or tell the truth?

In England they have a particular expression that fits this situation and would normally be uttered by Hugh Grant during a cheeky chappy moment in a romantic comedy. He would say "you are buggered".

Nowhere to run, nowhere to hide.

What is the equivalent of this in retail terms?

It comes as part of a, particularly ingenious, negotiation tactic.

If you wanted to lower the boom on a whole supplier base in one go, and watch the dollars pour in, a clever retailer could compose a press release that goes to all the industry magazines.

The headline might read something like this. *AnyMart* (fill in as applicable), *has completed an assessment and found that it is approximately 25% over-ranged.* Over-ranging is when you have too many products and lots of duplications. Basically you can run your business with a lot less items on the shelves. It is irrelevant to the results if it`s true or not.

So, what does this do? It sends your suppliers into panic mode. The first thing they know about this is when they read it in the papers.

There is then a speedy chain of events which often take place.

The initial thing that happens is the sales team get beaten up for not knowing what is going on with their customers.

The next thing that happens is that some senior director, maybe even the CEO, tears their shirt open to reveal the S logo on their chest. S in this persons mind does not stand for Superman, it stands for Super-salesperson. Actually it stands for Super-sucker.

Now they make the cataclysmic mistake. They phone the retailer and ask the question there will never be a good answer to. It is the commercial equivalent of the *does my bum look big in this dress*. That question is "Does this affect *our* products?"

Of course the retailer is going to suggest it does but there may be a good solution. Perhaps an idea would be a meeting to discuss it, but it should just be between the big kahunas. At this point you might as well put an apple in this persons mouth as the large pole is shoved up there rear end and they are put on the spit to roast.

Why do some senior executives think they know more than the people who run the business 24/7?

It always amazes me how much money is given away by *The Big Cheese* in a business. In the next chapter I will explain why this is so wrong.

Anyway back to the spit roast...

The meeting takes place between the senior person from the manufacturing company and the retailers representative. During the meeting a glorious solution is found. And the answer? More support to maintain the range. Brilliant!

Rule 7: Never believe that you are over-ranged. Your range is relevant to your discount and terms structure that has been negotiated over many years. As long as you've not allowed your brands to die on the vine, and become interchangeable, then be ready with a trading plan.

This broadside from a retailer often says "we have got it wrong and need more cash to hit our bonuses".

Trade your way to a bright new future. You are driving now. Focus on a spectacular outcome. The buyer will be under pressure from above to rake in as much cash from this tactical initiative as possible so fulfil their needs and fill your boots.

Mine are size 12 UK, size 47 EU and US 13. Big

boots hold a lot of money, and no they do not make my bum look big in this dress.

8 HIERARCHICAL NEGOTIATION
OR
"BIG CHEESE, BIG CHEESE GRATER".

So lets talk about big international organisations.

When it comes to negotiating with huge multinational companies you have to take a far more strategic approach.

If you work your way through any large international manufacturer you will find that, at each level, Managers, Directors, Vice Presidents and CEOs all have their own budgets and level of authority to make decisions.

Normally, the higher you go the less regard they have over the size of the money they sign off.

A Manager may well argue over hundreds or

thousands of dollars, a Director over tens of thousand and a CEO over millions.

Actually they all should be worried about cents if they have any sense (sorry the puns don't get any better).

Because they pay so little regard for sums, which they believe are insignificant in the scheme of things, it encourages retailers to negotiate with them.

Retailers are always negotiating. They never stop. Ever. Manufacturers mostly negotiate when they have something to sell.

Because it`s such a large part of a retailers life, they actively plan what their objective is for collecting cash over an annual period. Some even set cash targets for social occasions.

I have seen, first hand, millions of dollars lost by a manufacturer over a dinner table where they believe it is only a *fun evening entertaining a customer*. Best of all for the retailer, the manufacturer picks up the bill!

To be really effective though, you need to get serious. You need to get to grips with matrix selling. This is a process where you start by defining the question you want a *yes* to. Then you map out all of the relevant people in a retailers organisation and place them into a matrix. Next you highlight any who can impact on that *yes* and then put together a plan to positively align them before the question gets asked.

In this way you very rarely get a *no* because all the issues have already been dealt with.

Professional retailers do a similar exercise with manufacturers and pinpoint budget holders. In this way they understand where the cash is buried. Plans are then made to make certain these people are contacted by an appropriate member of the retail organisation, specifically with the objective of maximising the support they receive.

Does this work? Yes, brilliantly.

Sometimes writing your own books has its advantages because I can do something very selfish. In this case, thanking my old buying team. They were absolutely brilliant.

I have seen them work their way through events, held in beautiful locations and fabulous surroundings, where they professionally *schmoozed* around the room relieving suppliers of their profits.

And the best thing is that, the manufacturers loved the process and found it tremendous fun.

You see great retailers continuously sell. In fact the best buyers in the world are great salespeople. They sell manufacturers the idea that it is good to hand over buckets of cash.

When you marvel at how cheap food shopping is, don't necessarily thank the manufacturer. What helps keeps prices low is the skill of the buyers, who convince manufacturers to be over competitive, and who encourage them to find new ways of reducing cost of production, logistics, and ultimately accepting less profit than they would ideally like.

For retailers to make the massive profits, that many of them do, they have to fight as hard as possible to get the product on the shelves as cheaply as they can.

This means they become very inventive at finding ways to turn manufacturers upside down and shake all the money out of their pockets.

If you want to make a meal out of a *Big Cheese* you need a big cheese grater.

By complete luck, I bore witness to an international retailer making a snack out of *le grand fromage,* when I was still working for a multi billion dollar company that produce some very famous branded products. They will remain nameless, to save embarrassment, but I saw them fall for a masterful piece of smoke and mirrors negotiation.

A group of us had been summoned to an international marketing meeting which was being held in Europe. At one point the whole event was brought to a standstill and we had to pause discussions for a whole afternoon.

The head of commercial operations, who was attending our conference, needed to be excused so that he could meet the CEO of one of our largest international retail customers.

A day earlier, our global head office had been notified that the customer wanted an urgent face to face meeting with our *Top Brass*. To speed things up, we dutifully dispatched the corporate jet to pick them up and bring them from their country to our office. A nice touch I am certain they appreciated.

When they arrived they explained they were in a hurry because they had to visit another manufacturer, in a different country, later that day.

What they presented was a masterpiece of mental reasoning. They explained that, due to their growth, they now required a *Global Partner* for each category in their stores.

These partners would receive exclusive opportunities first, before any other manufacturer, and assist with strategic planning initiatives. In addition to this they would enjoy unprecedented access to the senior team on a regular basis.

To become a *Global Partner* it would only cost an additional 2% discount across the board.

In the space of 2 hours, 4 million dollars disappeared out of our profits. But not just this year, it was an annual discount and once given it is very hard to take back. Even more spectacularly, we not only used our jet to bring them, we then used it to take them to their next supplier meeting!

Now this deal may seem reasonable at first sight

but the reality is that it was just a way of justifying grabbing some more profit. In reality it just added more pressure to our business.

Over the years that followed, I never saw one single cent that came out of that deal which we couldn't have negotiated anyway. Not one.

Rule 8: Never have a CEO negotiate trade terms. It`s not their job. They have account managers to do that. Yes they should have an input behind the scenes but the account manager knows how the business is structured and where the details are. Good ones treat the money seriously because they have worked hard, over a long period of time, to get it. A CEO is too far removed from the day to day business and works in too large numbers to focus on small, but important, details. Good ones know this and let their teams do their job.

In the commercial jungle, the bad ones are the fatted calf ready for the slaughter.

If a retailer calls you and asks for a *Top to Top meeting*, the scraping sound you can hear in the background is probably the noise of a huge cheese grater being sharpened.

9 THREATS
OR
"WHAT DO SALES PIRATES DRIVE?"

Now after reading the previous chapters you may believe that retailers are devious, sneaky, tactical and down right untrustworthy.   To be fair, in some instances, you would be absolutely right.

However, it`s not surprising some of them resort to this, given some of the blaggs (English slang for robberies) that manufacturers pull.

Nowadays, there is far more legislation which regulates how retailers and manufacturers behave towards each other but for years different methods were used by manufacturers to coerce retailers into listing products.

Yes this is illegal in many countries, but I am going to guess that it still happens out there from time to time.

On a beautiful warm June day about 12 years ago, I had the pleasure to have a ringside seat on one of these spectacular occasions where the use of devious tactics went horribly wrong for one of my competitors.

At the time, I was looking after a retailer in the UK and had arrived early in the morning to attend a series of meetings with buyers, marketeers and logistics personnel, all of which were responsible for the products I supplied.

My day was half finished as I started the meeting with one of the logistics team.

Her desk was located in the centre of a large open plan office with the desks of many of the buyers located around it.

We were enjoying an easy going meeting as things, for once, were running as smooth as silk.

About 25 feet away one of the buying team had a relatively new, but very experienced, account manager in front of her and it looked like she was getting the full "have I got a deal for you" schpeel.

A look of unenthused boredom was firmly cemented to her face and I couldn't work out if it was real or just a ploy to help her negotiate a better deal.

In front of me the logistics person explained that the sales guy was from some market leading company. He was presenting a new range extension targeted to complement their existing products.

I said "She doesn't look impressed".

"No, she doesn't does she" replied the girl I was meeting.

We both watched for a minute because it looked

like he had wound up the presentation and was now asking for the order.

Sure enough she was shaking her head and giving him a flat *no*.

The next thing that happened surprised all of us in the office.

He sat back in his chair and spoke a few words quietly. In response she stood up and screamed at the top of her voice "HOW DARE YOU BLACKMAIL ME!"

There was silence all around us. The type of silence that feels really heavy. In fact this particular silence felt about the same weight as the W*orld Champion Hippopotamus Cheer Leading Team* as they successfully balanced themselves in a pyramid.

I watched as the buyer completely lost the plot. It is at this point I probably should have made a mental note not to marry her a few years later.

Looking at the startled face of the salesman suddenly reminded me of a song. To quote Debbie Harry "My man, your plan, backfired".

The silence was shattered by the next barrage he was on the wrong end of.

"GET OUT!"

Now in this situation there are eight words you

should never say and they are "I think you are over reacting, calm down."

Unfortunately he had missed this particular life lesson and his next mistake launched the situation into into the stratosphere. He actually said the fatal words "calm down" loud enough for everyone to hear. ALERT ALERT!

This led to a different level of screaming at a pitch that had dogs barking in adjacent countries.

With slowly increasing volume she pointed at the door and shouted "don`t... ...tell... ...me... ... to... ...CALM... ...DOWN... ...GET... ... OUT!"

At this point the Buying Director ran out of his office and asked them both to follow him back inside where things could be discussed quietly, behind closed doors. Unfortunately that door was partly glass so the heated discussion was plainly visible to everyone. Lip readers would have blushed.

After a while the account manager opened the door and walked to the exit. It was the most excruciating walk of shame I have ever witnessed as he shambled, head hung low, across the room and out of the door.

So what had he said that was so terrible it unleashed that level of venom?

Apparently, after he pitched the new product, the sales guy had been told by the buyer that there was no way she was going to buy these products.

At this point he obviously felt the pressure of having to tell his boss he was the only person in the team not able to get them listed.

This led him to make a mistake in the same league as Herr Hitler, believing that England would not be crazy enough to start a war if he decided to go on a jolly weekend outing across the border, and roll his tanks into Warsaw.

The salesman decided to leverage the strength of his other market leading range.

If he had sprouted a wooden leg, slipped on an eye patch and set sail in the good ship Black Banana, he couldn't have behaved any more like a Pirate.

He sat back in his chair and explained that, over the launch period of the new products, his company would have to prioritise who received stocks. Not only the new ones, but also the existing ones would be affected. In fact, only the people who supported his company by taking the full range of new items could be guaranteed stock of the old ones.

In effect, he had said that if she didn't list the new ones he would starve her of stock on the existing range!

Now one thing not to do is threaten a buyer commercially. In response to this she used the perfect weapon which all bullies hate. She made it public and called it what it was. Blackmail.

This is such a powerful word. When it`s used, the recipient reels backward from the impact like they have been hit by a cannon ball.

Rule 9: Never believe your own press. Just because you have the power, don't think you should ever use it on people you have to do business with tomorrow. Buyers will spend the rest of their careers extracting personal revenge. It`s not professional but, hey, most of them are only human.

In this case revenge came on speedy wings which were attached to some sharp claws.

Act like a Pirate and you will eventually walk the plank.

What does a Sales Pirate drive? A company caaaarrrrrrr!

10 INVOICE QUERIES
OR
"NEVER SHAKE HANDS WITH AN ANIMAL PROCTOLOGIST."

In many of these multi billion dollar businesses, there is a high level of complication.

Hundreds of products per supplier, individual terms per brand, promotional schedules run by many individuals, layers of discount by category, the list of ways you can get pricing wrong is amazing.

Many manufacturers have teams of customer engagement people focused at a single retailer, and in return the retailer has their own extensive team working with the supplier.

Gone are the days when one salesperson dealt with one buyer. Now business units have taken the place of these traditional one to one relationships.

This has exponentially increased the opportunity to cock-up pricing and support.

Some businesses maintain a reasonable control over this. They often use elaborate systems to track it but, because of the human factor, it can still go wrong.

Items change price on the wrong day, promotional payments start late, volumes are incorrect because of returns or failed deliveries. There are many reasons why this can cause problems and errors, inevitably, occur.

It can, in some instances, take weeks, months or years for them to become obviously apparent.

Combine with this the amount of correspondence sent between companies today, specifically due to the ease of contact via email, text or phone, and the problem magnifies when trying to trace the truth behind a specific issue. Especially if it`s highlighted many months after the event.

If there has been a change of personnel in that period, it can often be impossible to track the actual reality behind what has gone on.

In fact, this is a great opportunity for a retailer to pull yet another of their famous blaggs. The best thing is, this one actually sounds like they are being completely honest for once.

It is not uncommon for a manufacturer to receive a massive invoice from a retailer, sometimes for huge sums of money, to cover errors in invoicing and support payments. Accompanying the invoice is a note telling them that it will be deducted from the next monthly payment due.

Because manufacturers do not accrue funds for these eventualities it comes as a huge shock.

In fact, some of these claims can go back years (the furthest I have heard of is six) and cause chaos for the manufacturer.

The likelihood is that many can be explained and are not actually errors, but for others there is no traceability.

What many retailers do is bring in firms of accountants that charge a percentage based on the amount of money they eventually generate.

Other retailers bring in students during their summer break who are tasked with going back through records and looking for even the tiniest mistakes that might have been made.

The objective may be to overwhelm the manufacturer with data. In legal fights solicitors sometimes use a similar tactic when dealing with the opposing council. As part of the disclosure they send as much information as possible. A room full of boxes is delivered which makes finding the relevant information nearly impossible.

So when a manufacturer receives it, they often don't have the manpower to effectively trace all of the information in time. Ultimately what happens is that, they manage to track down some information and clear part of the invoice queries, but not all.

The remainder then becomes part of a negotiated settlement.

All of this seems perfectly reasonable doesn't it? Mistakes made should be rectified. All very legitimate. This is why so many companies and account managers have a problem with it. It's true they did make some mistakes, but here is why it is so tactical.

The retailer was never running the exercise to make certain *both* companies were treated fairly. This is not about fairness. It's about taking as much money from the other party as possible.

At no time did the retailer tell the people running the reconciliation to look for discrepancies for *either* side. They were only told to look for errors in the retailers favour.

If a manufacturer did this the retailer would scream blue murder, but the manufacturer is always worried about ruining the relationship, so it rarely happens.

Retailers, on the other hand, do not have the same concerns. They have no qualms about pulling stunts like this and, in the name of being conciliatory, manufacturers do very little about it.

Typically the outcome is this. If legitimate, the queries that can be traced will be payed, non legitimate ones will be discarded, and all remaining ones will be negotiated as part of a full and final settlement.

If the initial dispute is over $500,000 a manufacturer eventually paying out $100,000 will feel like they got away with murder. The retailer, who never stood to lose anything and to whom even $1 was a win, sits back and lights a large cigar.

All of this consolidation, invoice checking, internal paper audits and emergency meetings seems like a lot of work to go to for a manufacturer just because of a tactical stunt, dreamed up on the spur of the moment. There must me a better way to deal with it than this.

Rule 10: Invoice and support queries go both ways and should be dealt with as part of a joint consolidation of accounts. Both sides should share the cost and both should share the risk of finding they owe the other party some cash.

It may well be worth while putting this in the Terms and Conditions of supply along with a cut off date for back dating (where legal).

Actually, the best response I have ever heard of was from one member of a sales team being trained in negotiation.

During the course of the event one of the delegates received an email requesting payment of invoice errors totalling over $60,000.

His response was majestic.   He copied the information out of an email failure notice and then pasted it into a reply. It looked something like the one below.

Delivery to the following recipient failed permanently:

groupsnoreply@accountmanagerx.com

Technical details of permanent failure:
We tried to deliver your message, but it was rejected by the server.
The error that the other server returned was:
NICE TRY BUT STUPID REQUEST!

As he hit *send* he had an instant moment of panic. This was a big customer he was dealing with. What if he made them angry by not taking it seriously?

Within a minute his mobile rang with the buyers number showing on the screen.

He lifted it up and answered, worried about how angry his customer was going to be, and if he would still have a job at the end of the call.

On the other end of the line the buyer was laughing his head off.

The $60,000 disappeared over the course of the

call.

Why shouldn't you shake hands with an animal proctologist?

Well, if you are dealing with a customer who has spent the last few weeks going through the inside of a rats arse in the desperate hope of finding some easy money, you may want to think twice about shaking their hand.

You definitely want them to wash it first.

11 CASH MARGIN VS PERCENTAGE MARGIN
OR
"THE COMMERCIAL NINJA"

This is going to be short and sweet. An old friend of mine, Alan Mackley, who is a grand master of figure juggling, financial flim-flam and money manipulation, can spend days teaching manufacturers how to understand retail metrics. I don't want to get into that much detail here. What I would like to do is give a very clear overview of how figures can be used against a manufacturer.

A good way to illustrate this is to tell you a story about a product manager from my time in retail.

We had a supplier meeting to discuss promotional lines for the following six months and I was asked to sit in because it was being handled by their Commercial Director, and he expected, out of courtesy, to be met by a similar rank. The Commercial Director had been in the business for a decade, and was was perceived to be a very clever person.

Negotiating for us, on the opposite side of the table, was another very smart but relatively inexperienced 21 year old product manager.

She had been with the business a few months and was still finding her feet, but during that time she had worked with some good mentors in the team.

A meeting like this, between a junior member of a retailer and a very senior, experienced, business person, should have given the manufacturer a great outcome.

Actually things didn't quite work out that way. You see he had not realised she would come armed to the teeth. She brought with her the most devastating weapon in a retailers arsenal. A pocket calculator.

Over the previous months, working alongside the buying team, she had continually used it in anger. It had become glued to her. She never went anywhere without it. No person in retail attends an internal or external meeting without one.

I think some took it to the toilet with them out of habit.

Like anyone who uses a tool that often, she became an expert with it. It was like a Samurai Sword in the hands of a Ninja.

During the course of the meeting she ran numbers so fast that he couldn't keep up. Rather than admit he was not in the same league as her he allowed his ego to get the better of him and, after a few vague stabs at his dust covered calculator, he just agreed with everything she said.

It was carnage. In thirty minutes she took an extra $90,000 off him due completely to his inability to negotiate financially. In his terms, he saw it as a small percentage of margin and that is where the problem stems from.

This is the one thing that buyers always talk about.

If you ask them what their most important need is they will always say *percentage margin*. Just to be clear, this is rubbish. It may be a KPI but it is not the overriding business need.

Making 50% on $1 is not as important as making 2% $1,000,000. So why do they always say it is their biggest need?

Simple, because it easy to use to commercially disembowel an account manager.

If the retailer is making $7,000,000 dollars profit per year it sounds stupid for them to turn around and tell an account manager they need more margin.

If, however, they say I am only making 26% margin it sounds so much smaller.

This is why most retailers use margin on cost and not margin on markup.

Sorry to get technical but it is useful to understand how store prices are calculated.

If something costs $10 at cost and the retailer sells them for $30 that is a markup of 200%. Clothing retailers often use markup to set their pricing so that they can advertise 50% off and still make money.

They do not quote these to suppliers though. They quote margin as part of retail (less tax).   Sounds complicated but it is simple.   Something at $100 (excluding tax) with a cost of $40 is a 60% margin. It makes it look smaller.

Retailers especially do not talk cash. If the maths above was based on a sale rate of 10,000 per year it would be a cash margin of $600,000. It's not so easy to negotiate when you are already making significant cash margin.

"You are 2% under my average category margin" implies *the people in the woods* are giving the retailer more profit than this manufacturer.   It therefore sounds only fair to do the same otherwise you are uncompetitive.

The fact that *the people in the woods* are only delivering half the cash you are is lost (also assuming the buyer is telling the truth...). And yes I have had this one pulled on me personally. So have most of the salespeople I have trained.

Rule 11:   Cash is cash.   As Alan will tell you, everything else is smoke and mirrors. In a negotiation never let the money off the table. Talk in absolute values and avoid percentages (unless *you* are buying something of course).

Use a calculator instead of a spread sheet as often as you can to make certain you exercise the skill. Be a *Commercial Ninja*.

If you don't you may end up as commercial Sushi.

12 SEX
OR
"THE OLDEST PROFESSION"

So for a decade I have run sessions teaching sales teams how to maximise the impact they have with buyers.

To try to get things off the blocks in an interesting way I sometimes ask a simple question that gets people engaged.

That question is "What is the oldest profession?"

Typically there are a few smiles, an occasional look of *where is this going* and finally one person volunteers the word *prostitution.*

It`s funny the way they say it. Normally it`s a guy and he has that tone in his voice which makes it feel like he is implicated in the use of this particular profession just by knowing the answer, and speaking its name.

Anyway that`s not the correct answer.

Oldest professions in order:

First.   Sales.
Second.   Buying.
Third.   Everything else including prostitution.

A Profession is typically described as *supplying a service that requires direct and definite compensation for that specific event.*

Now we can argue until the organically fed, naturally reared, beef, comes wandering back to the farmhouse, about what constitutes a profession today, but I would put up a good argument for Sales and Buying to be included from the start.

They both have to be learnt if you are to be really good and schools teaching them are now scattered all around our world.

So my hypothesis is that, before a service can be undertaken or compensated it has to be sold and bought in that order.

Therefore, the answer to the time honoured question of which profession is the oldest is actually sales and not prostitution.

There is, however, a point at which the act of sex and prostitution does have a more intrinsic link between selling and buying. This is when the former delivers both of the latter.

I know this is going to be a very contentious subject but lets try to live in the real world and face some uncomfortable truths.

In the world of major retail and manufacturing large sums of money are traded everyday and, as I mentioned before, it is important for both sides to maximise the influence their relationships can deliver.

This leads to an interesting dichotomy. Businesses encourage salespeople and buyers to have close relationships so that they can leverage this to their own respective gain, but in the same instant they will see too close a relationship as breach of business ethics which could result in dismissal.

It obviously could lead to financial abuse, an anti-competitive advantage, and of course corruption.

In addition to this complexity it is completely illegal, in many countries, to choose buyers and account managers because of their sex.

This does not stop management from doing it. I have lost count of the conversations I have overheard through the years in which people are discussing who to put in charge of a particular account.

Comments like "We can't put her in charge, the buyers a woman, never put two women in a confrontational position" or "This guy is perfect, he will charm her" are common place.

It`s insane, illegal and infuriating.

Both sexes have their natural benefits in social situations but thinking this is the first criteria to consider when designing your team is about as backward as you can get, and it shouldn't happen.

It therefore seems it is an antiquated approach that has no place in today's business world and would infuriate either side of the equation.

But let's see what one of the groups affected has to say about it.

Bizarrely I have asked both male and female buyers what their opinion is and the majority respond in this way. "Actually as long as they do a good job I do not really mind if they are the same or the opposite sexual persuasion."

See, it doesn't matter!

If, however, you push them on the subject, they adapt their opinion slightly and say the *dynamics* are often better if the person is the opposite sex or similar sexual persuasion.

Dynamics is covert, politically correct speak for fun,

flirtatious, and far more interesting than any conversation can be in normal business meetings.

Add to this the high proliferation of both sexes in western commercial environments, plus continual travel and entertainment, then it mixes together to provide the basis for a highly charged busi-social opportunity to cross the line.

Trade conferences, awards dinners, factory visits, annual reviews, weekly/monthly/quarterly meetings plus the periodic team entertaining, delivers spectacular chances to take the business to the bedroom.

The stories are legendary.

Account managers attending meetings, secretly wearing the buyers underwear, which she gave him the night before.

Sexual prowess demonstrated at dinner (seriously I have never seen a wine bottle ejected from a cleavage before. It surprised me but scared the waiter so badly he nearly dropped the drinks tray).

Prostitutes, lap dancing bars, night clubs, private parties until the early hours, I have heard it all over the last 20 years.

Some industries are far worse than others. I have great sympathy for female account managers in some male dominated environments. During the evening they get parked next to the male buyers at dinner like they are being offered up as sacrificial lambs.

At some industry dinners the party moves to a strip club late in the evening and the women have two choices. Be packed off in a taxi back to the hotel because "this is men's stuff we are doing" or get dragged along to watch some drooling, sexually frustrated, muppet, run up an enormous bill which somehow ends up on an expense account.

If you think that sometimes this is needed to entertain clients, come out with my old colleagues for a night. We can show you how to run a wild event people will talk about for years, and not one naked woman needs to be involved.

Don't think it`s a one way street either. Female buyers can be just as bad, and I know several account managers who felt the need to "take one for the team" as they put it.

For those of you that do not work in these professions, it would probably shock you how much money is spent on customer entertainment either officially or unofficially.

Account managers can spend thousands each year entertaining their buyers. Corporately it may be tens of thousands per customer when the true cost is analysed, and globally the largest manufacturers will spend millions of dollars to make certain their retailers enjoy buying their products.

No it`s not seen as bribery (at least not in most of

the situations) it is just part of the game that is being played each day.

So with all of this interaction, it is no surprise that some relationships go way beyond the normal bounds.

The following story is urban legend now in an industry I used to work in.

A Managing Director sits in his office when one of his non commercial team leaders walks in and asks for a *quiet word* about something personal.

Behind the now closed door, the Team Lead explains that he is in a relationship with one of the buyers for a customer of theirs.

As they are both professional and there is no direct relationship between commercial entities the MD is not that worried and wishes them well.

Forward fast a year and the same MD has the head of his retail support team walk into his office and ask for a *quiet word*.

With a certain look of trepidation he says *yes* and the door closes again.

She explains that she is in a relationship with her direct counterpart at one of the largest customers they have.

Again he does not foresee a huge problem as these do not directly affect the negotiation of money between the two organisations, but now he is a little more uncomfortable.

Three months later an Account Manager, who looked after the same customer, walks into his office and asks for a *quiet word*.

Now if I had been the MD I would have been tempted at this point to say *no* but he was a better man than me, and instead invites him to close the door and sit down.

The Account Manager looks very worried but manages to tell his MD that he needs to make him aware of something.

He explains there is a slight issue with the account. He tells his boss that he is now living with the head buyer of one division!

At this point the MD, who is now wishing they were manufacturing guns so that he would have the opportunity to shoot himself, despairingly asks "what sort of business are they actually running over there?"

Rule 12: Don't forget the world of manufacturing and retailing is made up of real human beings. Getting surprised when relationships go to far is pointless. Until you have lived your own life fully and understand theirs completely, you have no right to judge or predict someone else's future.

You do, however, have a responsibility to deal with it. Businesses are successful because both sides invest passionately in doing a good job. If you make money out of the process you have a moral requirement to support people who get swept away by it.

If you manage a buying or sales team of 10 or more look around you. It is likely that at least one of these people has, is, or will be sleeping with a person from the other company.

How are you going to handle it if someone asks you for *a quiet word* and no, the answer is not to fire them? If this is the only threat they see you will never be told the truth and it will expose your business to real danger.

Have a clear plan in place to deal with it when it happens.

By the way. If the urban legend was actually true at least two of these people would end up getting married, and separately become responsible for at least one child and two very cute dogs. But only if it was true of course, which it obviously isn't...

13 TOTAL DE-LIST
OR
"DEFCON 1"

In the late 1950's, America looked to the world stage at the height of the Cold War.

It laid the global map out on the table and highlighted countries allied to its cause against the spread of communism around the world.

In front of its strategic leaders were very few locations that could easily give it extended reach into the Soviet Union for its long range ballistic missiles.

There were two, though, that jumped off the page as great sites to place nuclear warheads pointed at its old adversary.

Turkey and Italy presented themselves as geographically acceptable launch platforms.

Good weather, great beaches, fantastic food, half decent wine (well in Italy anyway) and within easy reach of strategic locations that needed to be blown to kingdom come if the ballon went up.

What more could you want? If you are going to war you might as well do it looking fab' with a George Hamilton sun tan, a slice of pizza in one hand, and a glass of Chianti in the other.

So by 1962 all seemed well and set for a summer of sun, sea, sand and strategic threats.

Unfortunately this didn't pan out exactly as planned. In Moscow the First Secretary of the Communist Party sat behind his desk deliberating the situation.

It had ticked off Nikita Khrushchev big style. Why should the Americans be able to get brilliant tans and do it in the name of a global arms strategy when he was stuck in Moscow freezing his rear end off for half the year.

Yes the Russian winter had helped save his mother country at least twice in this century from occupation by madmen bent on total domination, but it did not not help with his complexion at all.

He looked at a similar map of the world searching for some good weather, wonderful beaches and viable missile platforms.

After a few minutes the answer became obvious. Cuba was the perfect choice. Now a quick phone call to Fidel with a "have I got a great dealski for you" conversation, and he could start loading the boats with rockets.

This global escalation in the suntan race hit the Americans like a brick to the face. Cuba was 90 miles of their coast and the climate was even better than Italy in the winter time.

How could they allow Nikita to sit and develop a healthier tan nearly within sight of their shores. This was unacceptable on every level and to top it off he was bringing nuclear bombs with him!

In the Oval Office Jack Kennedy stared out of the window.

His campaign for President had been based on his movie star good looks and healthy skin.

It was obvious in every broadcast that America was the most dominant power in the world because he looked better on camera.

Now Nikita's plans would jeopardise this. He was out of control. If things continued this way the Russian leader could end up dating Marilyn Monroe for gods sake?

A picture of the screen goddess singing "Happy birthday Mr Premier" flashed through his mind.

Something had to be done.

In October the situation hit its peak. For 13 days US Navy ships blockaded Cuba and prevented the Russians landing with military supplies. On October 27th an American U2 spy plane was shot down by a Russian missile crew.

It marked the closest point the world has officially come to all out nuclear war. During the crisis

DEFCON 2 was declared for United States air command.

DEFCON stands for *defence readiness condition*. It denotes the level of alert to which the American forces are held at any one time. It has five increments with DEFCON 1 (exercise term "cocked pistol") signifying that nuclear war is imminent.

For two weeks in the late summer of 1962 the two most powerful nations on the planet took us closer to Armageddon than we have ever seen.

Eventually, a back channel deal was completed that involved the dismantling of weapons in Cuba, Italy and Turkey. The world breathed a sigh of relief.

It is difficult for us now to remember the near panic the world was in during those days. It seems detached and consigned to a moment of history that is impossible to re capture.

For some of us though, that shear panic does still happen today.

Imagine that you are the account manager of a multi million dollar business and your customer delivers over 20% of the organisations turnover and profit.

If your account stumbles, even for a short while, people in factories lose their jobs.

Maybe people sitting in the same office have to be

let go because profits fall.

Production costs are kept low by the scale of production that your account provides.

What then would happen if your customer took you to DEFCON 1?

Total all out war.

In retail terms this is called total de-list. Every one of your products is instantly removed from the retailers range. No warning, just no new orders.

Manufacturers never plan for this eventuality, and therefore do not have a contingency ready.

Overnight the cost of production of a single product can double making the rest of the business unprofitable.

It is a disaster which sends a business into meltdown.

But why and how could any retailer de-list an entire range from a major branded manufacturer?

Sometimes this game of chess has to be played for big stakes.

Even big brands like Coca Cola and Marlboro can be on the wrong end of a total de-list. In organisations this large they have the financial stability to weather the storm but many others do not.

In some notable situations, one country can be used as a piece on the chess board.

To prove a point a suppliers brands get de-listed in one country as part of negotiations in a much larger market. Again, punitive measures like these can be deemed illegal in some instances but, in reality, a retailer deciding to maximise its profit buy reducing suppliers is often a legitimate move.

Additionally, few manufacturers will complain to the authorities because they fear further retribution.

How can a retailer survive this and still hit its profit targets?

Actually it's more simple than it seems.

Products can be purchased through secondary supply channels, so the retailer still has limited product on the shelves, but what the manufacturer sees is its direct deliveries disappear.

Competitors of the affected supplier may be encouraged to increase support for their products which then covers the profit shortfall the retailer experiences. The competitors sales go up, especially for products that are largely substitutional such as chocolate bars.

Often the de-list is targeted to last a specific length of time which the retailer has budgeted for. Even short periods will have a massive impact with mid level suppliers.

But what triggers this behaviour? Often it is the supplier themselves.

They make, what they believe is a reasonable change in pricing in a market place and leverage their brand strength. This, because of market pressures to maintain a pricing position, means that the retailer loses cash margin. Margin they have not budgeted for.

It causes damage to the short term profitability of the retailer.

Sometimes the manufacturer believes that there is a chance for them to take a bigger share of the profit pie delivered by its products.

I have personally been on the wrong end of this and had one of the largest manufacturers in the world take away 3% of our profit at a time when it was critical to our business. Guess what happened to them 3 months later when we were unable to hit our targets without selling their products.

Manufacturers often take advantage of their position of power. What does this do? It makes them a target for a total de-list. To do this it takes a lot of planning, but eventually a retailer gets all its nuclear warheads pointed in the right direction and DEFCON 1 is declared.

Panic ensues, and now we are in the middle of the retail equivalent of the Cuban missile crisis.

How does this pan out?

If a manufacturer is sensible they hold firm, reduce overheads and makes a stand. It will often resolve itself within three months but they have to be prepared for the long haul just in case.

Better than this is not to get into the situation in the first place.

Suppliers who are always adding value for both businesses and continually generate new opportunities will, very rarely, be in this position. If, on the other hand, you believe you are all powerful and decide to remove profit from a retailer just because it is easy I can promise you will be taken to DEFCON 1 in the next year.

Rule 13: Managing a business is not enough. Driving the business forward is the only way to avoid total all out war. If you sit back and fall into the old trap of just managing the day to day of a large organisation you will eventually have war declared on you.

Set your ambition high, push the boundaries and design adventurous ways of delivering more value to both companies.

If you just fight over the current profit prepare for the red telephone to ring and Nikita to park nuclear warheads outside your office.

14 DISUNITY
OR
"WITH FRIENDS LIKE YOU WHO NEEDS ENEMIES"

Buyers are predators.

Predators, whether they are sharks, lions or any other beast that preys on others, very rarely attack the strongest animals in a group.

It doesn't matter if it is a herd of antelope or school of fish, they tend to focus their attention on the weakest rather than pick a fight with the toughest adversary.

Buyers are no different. They have a natural instinct when it comes to selecting their prey and will go after those they feel are easy marks. They are also opportunists.

If a chance arises it is very difficult for them not to take the initiative and feed on the poor unfortunate lame individual in front of them.

Let me give you an example. I will tell you the story of when I got separated from the herd, so to speak.

New born animals are often targeted by predators, and in the commercial world their equivalent is a new salesperson taking over an account.

Still finding their feet they can be easy pickings for experienced buyers.

My particular experience happened when I had just taken over managing a large customer for my employer at the time.

Over several meetings I started to establish some sort of rapport with the buyer, but things took a significant downturn during an annual range review.

We had scheduled a meeting at my head office and were running through the range to select products for the next promotional period.

Everything was going well up until, my then boss, decided to *help provide me with some support.*

He was a great guy but totally underestimated the particular dangers negotiating with the predator I had in front of me.

After popping in to meet the buyer, and demonstrating how much we valued their business by asking very studious questions, he decided to check on how well the new boy (me) was managing to service their needs.

"Is Mark looking after you ok?" He asked the buyer.

"Yes he's doing a good job." The buyer replied smiling. "No problems at all".

"Well here's my card if you get any problems." My helpful and concerned boss says as he stands up to leave.

In this one simple unobtrusive act I was separated from the herd, and now placed squarely on the menu.

I could virtually see the drool forming in the buyers mouth as he realised there was a total lack of unity in our business.

Sure enough, about twenty minutes later, we got into a heated discussion about the invoice price of a new product we were introducing.

I refused to cave in to his pressure to simply reduce the price without some sort of trade, and this turned into a Mexican stand off.

The room went quiet for several minutes. Then, very deliberately, the buyer leaned back in his chair and said "You know I told your boss you were doing a great job? Perhaps I need to call him and tell him you are not doing such a good job now..." In front of me my bosses business card was being waved casually back and forth.

Rule 14: Never, ever, forget that the pleasant buyer in front of you sporting a happy smile is actually a ravenous killing machine.

Stay unified. You are only strong as part of the herd. You may look in the mirror and believe you are a lion ruling the savannah but actually, on your own you are a gazelle, the animal kingdoms equivalent of a bargain bucket at Kentucky Fried Chicken.

15 NO
OR
"WHAT IS THE SOUND OF SILENCE?"

One of the best negotiation *professors* specialising in the world of FMCG is a guy called Steve Boyce.

Steve has a great way of getting across the simplistic nature of professional buyers.

An ex buyer himself, he is brilliant at using the most minimalist skills to his advantage.

One of his famous quotes deals with the way a buyer uses two simple elements and combines them to devastating effect.

As a salesperson winds up their pitch and asks for the order Steve just says "No", and then goes quite.

After the silence builds for a few seconds, the salesperson, who is pre-programmed to ask questions and find solutions, steps straight into the beautifully constructed and elegantly simple trap.

The sales person says one word... ..."why?"

At this point Steve reels off a long list of spurious, but plausible reasons why the deal isn't good enough.

In true super salesperson mode the poor individual utters the classic sales pre-close "so if it wasn't for these problems we could do the deal?"

Steve concedes that there is a chance and immediately the salesperson starts shedding cash desperate to add more value to make the deal work.

Eventually there is nothing left to give, and at this (and only this point) the deal is done.

Steve's classic quote is, in the unlikely event that he gets bored with teaching account managers to negotiate, he will open up a school of buying. In it he will only teach two things, *how to say no and how to go quiet*.

Buyers revel in silence. It is their old friend and it makes them easy money.

No and *go quiet*. **Just the combination of the two will make a fortune for any retail business. Try it yourself. When you next go to buy a car or any other capital goods just wait for the** salesperson to go for the close and say *no*, then just start thinking of anything. The shopping, what's on TV that night, anything that keeps you from saying a word.

Within a minute you will get a "so what are your concerns" comment. At that point you explain you aren't happy with the colour, size, delivery date, pattern of the the salesman's tie, hairstyle of the saleswoman, really anything at all and finally, of course, the price.

Please send me 10% of everything you get as a discount and I will buy my own island in a year.

Rule 15: The word "no" from a professional buyer is not an answer it's the start of a negotiation. Understand that most of the time it means "yes", but I need to know I am getting your best deal".

This is unless you have a useless, uncompetitive and, more importantly, substitutional product. If you are working for a company that keeps bringing these to market you may want to re-evaluate your career decision.

What is the sound of silence?

For buyers it is the sound of money fluttering out of an empty sky.

16 TEAR UP THE AGENDA
OR
"THE WINDOW LICKER ON THE BUS"

I was talking to a friend of mine who had just spent a week in Hamburg, Germany and had to experience the wonderfulness of its public transport system, specifically the buses.

In general Hamburg has a good infrastructure with great rail links into the city but what fills the gap between locations are regular bus services that have to be experienced to be believed.

I have always marvelled at the ability of public transport to attract a special level of crazy person, but for some reason buses in particular have cornered the market on "window lickers" as another friend describes them.

This is not a description of people who have to deal with life while struggling with real mental issues, it rather describes the people who just have a different take on the world around them.

Personally, I believe life would be so much less colourful without the truly eccentric who spend their time looking at the world through a slightly different porthole than the rest of the human race. From time to time, I believe my friends place me firmly in this category of individual so I have a natural empathy for them. Comrades in arms in our quest to make those around us uncomfortable with the neat world they have constructed inside their tidy heads.

With so many people like this, and the polarising effect buses have on this group, it was not surprising that, on her daily trip around the streets of Hamburg, she would come across one of those wonderfully colourful individuals. Someone who was making life more interesting in a simple, but beautifully random way.

This particular social magician took the form of an ordinary looking thirty something man dressed simply in drab greys and blacks, as most people in Hamburg seem to do during the winter.

The ability to be impervious to colours outside the grey spectrum seems to be a special skill particular to Hamburg people in general. Just as bullets bounce off the Man of Steel, colours seem to ricochet off Hamburgians, and this particular citizen on the bus was no different from his fellow neighbours.

He had realised that a typical journey lacked any real appreciation of its complications. Taking a ride on public transport was taken far too much for granted, and he was making it his mission in life to show his appreciation for each travellers achievement when they successfully managed to buy a ticket, board the vehicle without injury, and eventually secure a seat.

As they made their way into the bus from the door, he exploded in rapturous applause only letting it subside when they had made it into their desired seat unharmed.

Occasionally he paused as the person hesitated, partly due to the shock of the noisy welcome, partly due to their desperation to find somewhere to sit as far away from him as possible. As soon as they continued their journey, and bottom met vinyl, the applause would start again until he felt they were suitably acknowledged for not spontaneously combusting before they completed the difficult task in hand.

At no time did anyone ever attempt to talk to him or ask why he was doing it. This inability to face extreme and unusual behaviour, in a relatively normal environment, lends itself to another spectacular tactic that retailers use to take command of an agenda, It turns a simple meeting into an opportunity for gain.

The pressure on manufacturers salespeople, to secure listings for new products that are launched, can be extreme. Imagine your company has invested a huge amount of money designing a new range of products and it is your responsibility to get it listed in one of the larger national retail chains.

Millions of dollars ride on your ability to convince the buyer to select your product for inclusion in their range. It is not surprising then that a lot of effort and preparation is put in prior to the meeting where the products are *sold in.*

Sometimes the planning can take days to put together, and involve a large team including Marketeers, Account Managers and Directors.

When a retail buyer or category manager gets the phone call to arrange a meeting to present the product, many go into high gear ready to build a strategy to get the best terms for the new potential listing.

But what happens if the product is so good that the buyer has no choice but to buy it. This doesn't give the retailer much chance for negotiation. Enter the *Window Licker* approach!

Typically the sales team (maybe an Account Manger and their boss or a Marketing Manager) turn up to present and are shown into a meeting room to await the retailer.

In walks the buyers and they sit down ready for the manufacturers to start. This takes the form of a statement of the agenda the salespeople have scripted for the meeting. Typically a copy is printed and handed over for both sides to agree before the meeting gets going. It may even have been sent in advance.

It`s at this point that the trap is sprung.

A member of the buying team, normally the senior person, goes off the reservation.

He or she picks up the beautifully prepared agenda, which has the new product launch right at the top, and slowly tears it up in front of the salespeople's eyes.

They then proceed to blow a gasket and start an insane tirade about the manufacturer always working for their own self interest, never understanding the retailers problems, and not focusing on the real issues, (which incidentally suddenly include low margins, rubbish logistics, and crap products).

Before the manufacturer can work out which way is up they are told to leave and get their business in order before they talk about any new product.

It is a masterful stoke of lunacy that most manufacturers think is real, even if they don`t understand what is going on they certainly are not going to argue with a completely mad person who is frothing at the mouth like a rabid squirrel.

Before they go they are told to come back with a plan that starts with ways they can drive the current business and then, and only then, will they be allowed to discuss the new range.

Now the agenda is the retailers not the manufacturers. Corporate confidence in the sales team is crushed and it would take the mental strength of Houdini to return without sharpening your pencil on the cost prices of the new range.

Rule 16: Everything that happens on the run up to a selling meeting is an act. It is the retailers way of pre-conditioning your mental state so that you feel at your most compliant and conciliatory.

If you walk into a meeting, and in the first few minutes the *window licker* appears just remember it is not really a crazy person, it is a actor... ...unless the meeting is in Hamburg of course and he starts applauding as you walk in.

17 POWER PLAY
OR
"A SHOT IN THE GREASY GRASS"

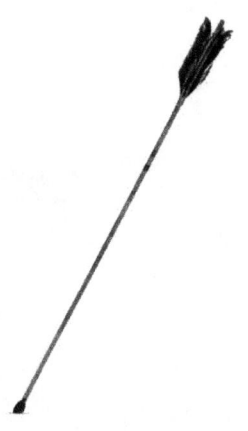

The Greasy Grass River, as it is known to the Lakota Indians, meanders through the Montana countryside over several miles and is surrounded by rolling hills.

It hasn`t changed dramatically over the last one and a half centuries, so if you walk through the fields surrounding it today you can still get an idea of what it looked like back then, the smell of the grass and the sounds of the wind across the fields.

If you had been alive on June 25th 1876, and were standing on one of the surrounding bluffs, you would still recognise the same scene that lay in front of you.

Today you may notice a new road or building in the distance, but most of it would be familiar. What would be missing from the panorama would be an Indian village two and a half miles away with the dust rising as many ponies were being taken to graze for the morning.

Even from that distance, you would have been able to make out women busying themselves for the day ahead...

...The village was large. Larger than Mitch Bouyer,

the Indian scout watching from the hill, had ever seen before. In the thirty years he had been around these tribes he had come across every manner of settlement but none that rivalled this.

He had been expecting eight hundred or so Native Americans to make up the group but it seemed like there were far more ponies than he would have imagined necessary for such a small force.

Bouyer made his opinion known, but was unable to convince the others in his party, that the numbers didn't make sense.

What they did not know was that their original information was wrong and that, missing from the headcount in front of them and making it appear lower than reality, were many of the men.

They were still sleeping from the previous evening and this gave a false impression of the numbers viewed from that far away.

The small group on horseback rejoined the rest of the party which now totalled around two hundred and ten.

Their orders were clear, they were there to force the Indians back to the reservations, and the Lieutenant Colonel leading this part of the ground force intended to follow them through. He was, at this point, particularly concerned that the village was about to be alerted to their presence. This would make the job of rounding up the *hostiles,* as they were classed, far more difficult as they dispersed.

He had, therefore, made the decision to attack a day earlier than he wanted to so that he retained the element of surprise. This meant that he hadn't have time to scout the area properly.

Beyond the Lieutenant Colonels view, ten thousand Native Americans, including up to three thousand warriors, began their day unaware that the soldiers were heading towards them.

He studied the map and traced his finger along the river and down the valley. It didn`t show the Lakota Indians name for it. Instead it just said two words. "Little Bighorn".

Away in the distance, George Armstrong Custer`s objective for the day was a group of Indians led by a great Chief.

Unbeknown to the 7th Cavalry leader, Sitting Bull had amassed many warring nations into one unified force. The Lakota had been joined by the Northern Cheyenne, and Arapaho. All of these swelled the numbers beyond belief.

In charge of one of the largest war parties was Chief Crazy Horse. His reputation was fierce and well deserved. He had led many successful raiding parties and believed himself to be protected by the great spirits in battle. When he was younger, his father had taken him on a vision quest. Legend has it that the two warriors were shown the way to its location by a red-tailed hawk. There he entered the world of the spirits, and they made him a gift of a medicine bundle which would protect him for life.

As Custer set off towards the village a shadow briefly fell across his face. Overhead, a red-tailed hawk circled. Intermittently, its outstretched wings put the calvary column into eclipse. It was watching their steady advance down the valley.

Now the rest of what happened is somewhat open to debate, and probably only the hawk knew exactly what happened next, but here is my version of events.

We do know that at some point both sides saw the other. I am guessing that the responses were as follows.

Indians: "Look! Here come some soldiers, let's go say hello."

Custer: "Holy crap, where did all those Indians come from?"

Now I think everyone knows how the story ends. Over 200 cavalrymen lost their lives due to the overwhelming force they were facing.

You may wonder why I am drivelling on about yet another page in history. Well there are two reasons. First, this chapter would be far too short and dull if I didn't pad it out with something slightly interesting.

Second, retailers re-enact Custer's Last Stand on a regular basis.

I don't think there is one Account Manager that hasn't walked into a meeting, expecting to find one person inside, but discovering the whole Indian Nation waiting the other side of the door.

If the poor salesperson realised that the words that go through their mind as they enter the meeting, "holy crap, where did all those people come from", are virtually the same as George Armstrong Custer they would probably join the dots as to what`s going on.

No salesperson would ever turn up at a meeting with several colleagues in tow without telling the retailer in advance. They believe that it is just common courtesy to announce it prior to the event, and also their customer would get really annoyed if they were blindsided like this.

Retailers, on the other hand, are related to Crazy Horse. They know that it is extremely intimidating when they turn up mob handed to meetings unannounced.

Rule 17: When you arrive at a meeting and there are the commercial equivalent of ten thousand Native Americans in full war paint waiting for you, walk through the door and scream "Ambush!"

If they don't laugh at that then ask them if they are in the wrong room and that you believe Custer is next door waiting for them.

Do not be polite and say nothing, it's a tactic. You should understand that, and they have to know that you know that they know that you know that...

18 PRICE INCREASES
OR
"HEADS I WIN TAILS YOU LOSE"

The man sitting at the table opposite me was remarkably unremarkable.

If the police had asked someone for his description the one word that would have been used was *average*.

Average height, average weight, average hair length, average age, average sun tan... ...average. In fact he did *average* in a less than average way.

He was superb at it without trying, genetically gifted in the art of being the median for a white male.

I knew that it must have been a disguise as soon as I realised he was perfectly ordinary, too perfectly ordinary.

Like Superman, he used his anonymity to hide his real identity. Sitting less that eight feet from me, sipping an expresso, was a Superhero and like all Superhero's he only revealed himself when a threat to the innocent or an opportunity to do good presented itself. What happened in the next few minutes tore away the mild mannered, average, exterior to expose his true alter ego.

As we sat, roughly facing each other, we made eye contact and gave a nod of acknowledgement. Both giving appreciation for two men who had discovered the art of enjoying a solitary coffee in a french café bathed in the sunshine of a warm autumn afternoon in Paris.

The Wayfarers we both wore suggested a camaraderie that comes from recognising similar tastes in a fellow member of the Club Human. A special, members only tribe that delineated itself by an unwritten rule of hedonistic love of life.

Card carrying, dues paid, blood let, we both understood what it meant to achieve inclusion in the oldest private members affiliate in the world.

For a moment I believed we were equals, but I was wrong. Within a moment I realised I was an amoeba compared to his level of evolutionary development.

My clarity of understanding, about his true nature, was delivered by the footsteps I could hear walking towards us.

Over his shoulder my attention was stolen, without any objection, by an oncoming tsunami of womanhood.

She was, what a friend of mine simply describes as, elegant. Not just well styled, but something as far removed from average as light glinting off coal is from the translucent sparkle a diamond delivers from exactly the same ray. The basic ingredients are there, but producing an altogether different result.

She was Audrey Hepburn dressed in Chanel elegant. Catherine Deneuve, playing a timeless vampire in The Hunger, sexy. Catwalk chic, with style oozing from every pore. Dressed for a funeral but invited to a party. Only Parisian woman seem to effortlessly achieve this mix of femininity and strength.

Look at todays political landscape in France. Since Joan of Ark it has been waiting for a woman to step forward and lead her country into their bright new future.

Unfortunately the sad array of weak, sad, inept men who have peppered her history by buying their way into power, have diluted Frances true potential and opened her vein allowing lifes blood to ebb out into the streets.

They are nothing like the woman that had just arrived.

Have you ever been in a room full of people idly chatting when someone enters who seems to have their own gravitational field. Not generated by rank, but by calm self assurance.

This was what had now taken its seat on the adjacent table to our superhero, but there was a flaw in the stone.

As the waiter approached, she lifted the Jackie O sunglasses which were shielding her eyes. It was a gesture of polite courtesy towards the waiter which was unnecessary, but appreciated. She ordered an expresso. Her eyes flashed into view. They were dark, black as a moonless night in the forest, filled with emotion, and visible only for a second before the shades slid back into place.

Sometimes you have the privilege of being part of someones life when you can make a real difference, and that's where my new acquaintance found himself in this moment.

It would have been easy to either miss the look in her eyes or decide that it would be too much trouble to get involved, but he was too observant and not afraid to take a risk.

He looked across, let the waiter return with her coffee, allowed him to deposit the tiny cup, and return to the kitchen before he spoke.

His voice softly broke the silence with an

unmistakable American, Deep South accent that filled the air like poured honey fills a jar.

"Excuse me Ma'am I don't want to intrude but I just wanted to ask a question if that's ok?" he said.

Her accent was warm, and clear, and rich. It sounded like sad music. "Sorry but I am not in a very talkative mood today" she said.

A tear edged under the rim of her glasses and stained her cheek. It was rimmed with a faint trace of mascara but nothing that left a noticeable trace on her milk smooth skin.

His voice softly continued in spite of her reply. "I was just sitting and wondering, what would be the right one?"

She turned. "The right what?" she asked.

He stared into the distance and soaked up the pale orange sunlight that artists of the left bank made their trade. "The right music".

She stared at him and asked impatiently "The right music for what?"

"The music that would fit this moment, now, here, for you?" He replied as he turned from the sun towards her. His face, now illuminated by her instead of the sun, she actually seemed to increase its radiance.

"What makes you think there is any that would be

in my mind?" She said.

"Mine would be *New York State of Mind*." He said ignoring her question.

She paused and then asked "We are in Paris, it's beautiful, why would you want to be in New York?"

"Sometimes some things, however stunning they are, do not fill you with what you need" he said "New York fills me."

She was thoughtful for eight, nine, ten seconds and then started to sob uncontrollably.

Through the tears she managed to say *"Here in the dark, in these final hours, I will lay down my heart and I'll feel the power."* The last words were punctuated with snatched breaths and then she stopped, unable to continue. The air fell silent apart from her continued gasping between tears.

He picked up the lyrics and finished *"But you won't, no you won't, 'cause I can't make you love me, if you don't."*

In a steady movement he stood, closed the distance between them, sat, and folded her into his arms. She clung to him as if hanging from a cliff, and he was the only thing between her and a plummet into the unknown.

Every ounce of emotion, trapped behind her eyes, flooded onto his shoulder.

Over the next thirty minutes I was transfixed by the gradual change in her physical and mental demeanour. She started out exhausted from the release of emotion which had obviously built over a considerable time. Her body had lost its grace and strength, she had become tiny and frail.

But time and care can sometimes change people quickly. By the time the two had finished their third coffee she looked relaxed, rejuvenated, refreshed. Life radiated through her skin again. She now shone bright as a solar flare.

They talked of loves lost and found, of life's cruel twists, and fates wicked humour. Of the hearts fallibility in its inability to choose rationally. Finally they talked of nothing serious, good coffee, bad restaurants and beautiful art.

Eventually the conversation and the laughter subsided and they just sat, comfortable with the silence between them.

And then it was over. She asked for the bill, he insisted on paying. Goodbyes were said and hugs exchanged and then she was gone.

No second meeting was arranged, no telephone numbers asked for or given. They would, most likely, never see each other again.

I had to leave too, but as I turned and walked away something stopped me. I walked back to his table and said "Excuse me, I saw what happened just now, can I ask you a question?"

"Yes if you want to" he smiled.

"Why did you get involved? What was in it for you?"

"It's simple really" he said "I had two choices. Take a risk and attempt to help someone who was in need, or ignore it and carry on with my coffee. As I see it getting involved would then have two possible outcomes. One, she would tell me to get lost. Two, was just what happened. I helped her past what was causing her so much pain. Whichever I chose, I would have known that I had at least tried. Either way I feel I did the right thing, so there was nothing for me to lose. Heads I win tales you lose."

"In fact" he continued "I would only lose if I did nothing because I know I would regret it later. The way it worked out, she feels unburdened and free to think clearly. I feel like I can look at myself in the mirror with a clear conscience."

Like a true Superhero after the danger has passed he slipped back into his alter ego, and blended back into the crowd, job done, back to anonymity, seeking no award or tribute.

His logic was perfect, unbreakable. On the face of it it seemed like a risk but, in reality, he could not lose unless he failed to try.

In commercial situations it can also be the case that, what seems on the surface to be a risk is, actually, a no brainer when you understand what the real consequences are.

An example of this are price increases.

One of the most hated tasks any salesperson has in their list of duties is putting through increases in the cost of a product.

Why is it such a loathed part of their job? Well, it's partly due to a lack of understanding about what happens when a manufacturer increases their invoice price.

Because retailers are so focused at getting costs down salespeople believe that a price increase is something that the buyer is going to hate. This is not necessarily the case. Actually, the only person who should hate prices increasing in general are shoppers themselves. But let's face it, if all toilet roll prices go up in every store nearby you are not going to give up using it (or at least I hope you don't). No, you just accept that it is the price of a basic commodity you consume. Retailers call these types of products daily staples. They include things like bread, cheese and milk.

What buyers often want to achieve is the maximum cash profit from each product they have in their stores. Keeping prices low is not necessarily the best way to achieve that. They really want to have the same or, better still, slightly lower price than their main competitors.

This money, in very basic terms, is generated by the volume of the product, times the money it makes for each unit sold. Charge more, reduce the cost, increase the volume and the total goes up. Sometimes actually reducing the price can sell so many more that it also increases the total profit.

Whatever way you maximise the cash you eventually get to a point, particularly in established markets, where the pricing finds its optimum position against the competition.

This is a massively simplistic view of pricing because it is actually far more complicated the deeper you get into it, but this covers the basics. Now, if you are a manufacturer and you want to make more money and costs of production and delivery is as low as you can get it then you have to consider a price increase.

Sometimes it is necessary for prices to go up to cover a raw material cost increase. When this happens you hope that your competitors will follow you knowing that they too can make more money or at least not reduce what they already make.

In reality, pricing should be set independently of competitors. However, if you look at some markets, as the market leader puts prices up, for whatever reason the rest will often follow relatively quickly.

So the ideal scenario, for any manufacturer wanting to increase profits, is to increase its pricing and then for all its competitors to immediately increase retail prices. Finally, for it to work perfectly, all its retail customers need to do exactly the same thing.

In this way the manufacturer sells the same amount at a slightly higher price and so do all the other suppliers. A good result for all of them but not for the shopper.

Here is where the wheel often comes off. Firstly it is illegal, in many countries, to *fix* retail pricing if it eliminates competition. This makes sense, as it should provide retailers the chance to sell at whatever price they want.

If, however, a retailer does not increase its price on a key product every other retailer will want to match that price too to stay competitive.

This puts a massive strain on the manufacturer for several reasons.

First they have just taken margin away from the retailer, which is never a good place to be unless you are massively dominant in a market (and even then it royally hacks them off).

Secondly, in some markets a manufacturer may come under extreme pressure to compensate a retailer for loss of profit until the price goes up in every store.

Now this *really* is illegal in most developed markets. Does it still happen? Probably yes, some will do a back door deal that increases promotional support while the instability continues in its market pricing.

Failure to do this may cause reprisals such as de-listing or removal from key positions in store.

All of these painful scenarios await a salesperson who is told to jack up the invoice price. Basically they spend most of their time developing good relationships with their customers only to have all their hard work sabotaged, as they see it, by an increase in prices.

The funny thing is that retailers often like price increases, especially in static markets (although they will never tell a manufacturer this).

Why is this the case? Simple, retail sales targets go up like the sales targets the manufacturer has. Manufacturers often concentrate on volume sales but retailers focus on cash through the till.

So in many retailers, if prices go up and they maintain their percentage margin, their cash sales and profits increase!

As long as the whole market goes up and sales rates maintain they are quids in.

What they tell the salesperson is different though because a buyer wants to not only maintain margin, but they actually want to increase it. So they lie. They complain. They tell manufacturers salespeople that it is not fair to the shopper. That the market is too tough to take a price increase. All of these things are about making certain they get the best deal for themselves.

Actually, behind the scenes, many of them are extremely happy that prices have gone up. Why? Retailers talk percentage margin all the time. Say a retailer makes 20% margin on a product that sells for $100 i.e. $20. Now the manufacturer puts up the cost price by 10%, so it now costs $88 for the retailer to buy. If they apply their typical 20% margin it now sells for $110, but instead of making $20 it now makes $22. As long as the volume stays the same it has increased its cash profit without doing anything.

If this happens on something like a box of cereal, which retailers sell millions of each year, you can only guess the impact it makes to the bottom line.

The retailer may also try to increase the percentage margin they make, even though they already make more cash out of the increase than the manufacturer.

Rule 18: Price increases are not always bad news to everyone with one exception, the shopper. If you are the person that is parting with your money each week you are the one that feels the pain.

Retailers, on the other hand, do not lose out as long as they remain competitive and are not unfairly disadvantaged in the market place.

Heads I win, tails you lose.

19 THE END
OR
PERHAPS JUST A NEW BEGINNING

For a hundred thousand years, people who grow food or produce products have traded them to consumers.

It has only been in the last few thousand years that the concept of retailing and manufacturing has developed into something we recognise today.

Shops have now been developed based on the requirement that the transactions should occur in a geographical location which is convenient to the consumer.

In the next decade this will end.

Barriers to internet trade will fall away.

Your local store will be in your pocket and delivery will often be within minutes, not days.

How will this change the world of buying and selling?

The truth is I don't know, but I can guarantee one thing. The game will continue, and that`s good.

It may take some time for retail to re-adjust, and many household names will fail the test, but the ones that survive will produce a new, exciting, experience for shoppers to enjoy.

Retailers and manufacturers will need to re-invent themselves to compete, and in that revolution the pressure for cost efficiency will be more extreme than ever before.

Buyers will be more inventive, salespeople better skilled, and shoppers more demanding.

It`s going to make for some interesting meetings.

I can't wait.

BOOKS BY MARK TAYLOR

Humour

Puppy Tales and Cocktails

An irreverent, laugh out loud, guide to surviving the first 30 days of owning a puppy.

When a puppy appears on an 11 year old boys wish list his father deals with the problem like any rational man.

He starts making cocktails.

Puppy Tales and Cocktails *Remixed*

The follow up to *Puppy Tales and Cocktails* in which Una the dog gets to tell the story from her point of view and she doesn't pull any punches.

It's a story of cocktails, cock-ups and cats, which will make you laugh all the way to the bar.

Puppy Tales and Cocktails *The Sock Thief*

(Imminent release).

Time has moved on and so has the puppies wardrobe.

A new level of anti social behaviour has appeared and is causing chaos in the apartment.

On top of this several excursions have turned into a complete farce, and something has to change or it's *Taser time for the Terrier.*

General interest

Who Killed Category Management

Ever wondered how drastically your future will be affected as internet shopping takes hold?

Who Killed Category Management lays out the problems all of us will face and shows why everyone should be worried how retailers adapt to the oncoming tornado that is touching down around us.

Fifty Shades of Shopping Un-gagged

Deception, lies, abuse, sex, blackmail, intimidation.

For some people working in retail and manufacturing industries, this is a typical day at the office.

Fifty Shades of Shopping Un-gaged lifts the secret veil which covers the dirty, sneaky and downright funny behaviour, some businesses use to make money out of your weekly shopping trips.

If you are in sales, buying or indeed a shopper, this will change the way you view the world around you.

ABOUT THE AUTHOR

Mark has had a bizarre career which has taken him around the world.

He has spent his life in commercial FMCG roles both in Manufacturing and Retail. More recently he also specialised in people development including Leadership programs.

During his career he acknowledges he has been very lucky to have worked with some exceptional professionals who have helped shape his life.

These have enabled him to enjoy success across diverse industries including Alcohol, Fashion, Electrical, Confectionary, Grocery, I.T. plus many others.

He specialises in negotiation, sales, buying, commercial strategy, marketing and teaching but he holds a special place in his heart for boat rocking with a smattering of tree shaking.

He now spends his time working with organisations that want to move their people, business and commercial results forward by delivering something really special for their customers.

As you will notice from the book, his style is very straight forward and he values partnerships that seek the truth, not just a sugar coated pill to massage egos. Life is just too short for that.

An accomplished public speaker he also enjoys key note opportunities. If you need your audience to be challenged, to think differently about manufacturing and retail, he is guaranteed to create a platform for discussion.

He now lives in Switzerland, where he holds the record for most Fondues eaten in a year.

Make some magic happen.

www.whokilledcategorymanagement.com